National Theatre Plays Series

LOST WORLDS

Newsflash
Wedding Breakfast
Roost

by

WILSON JOHN HAIRE

HEINEMANN
in association with the National Theatre
LONDON

Heinemann Educational Books Ltd
LONDON EDINBURGH MELBOURNE TORONTO
JOHANNESBURG NEW DELHI AUCKLAND
SINGAPORE HONG KONG NAIROBI
IBADAN KUALA LUMPUR KINGSTON

200 306 424

ISBN
0435 23363 7

822 HAIR

First published 1978

Applications must be made in advance to:
Margaret Ramsay Ltd
14a Goodwins Court, London WC2

Published by
Heinemann Educational Books Ltd
48 Charles Street, London W1X 8AH
Set in 10/11pt Garamond by
Spectrum Typesetting, London
and printed in Great Britain by
Biddles of Guildford

INTRODUCTION
by
John Russell Brown

Wilson John Haire's latest play is going to puzzle all the cataloguer. So few contemporary dramatists write good parts for actresses, or open a woman's view upon the world, that LOST WORLDS is most likely to be categorised, with gratitude, as a full-length play '1 m; 8 f' — although to be fully appreciative a note should add that 'with doubling it could be 1 m; 5 f'. But another cataloguer might place this work in the 'One Act Play' division under three different titles, for each of its three parts is complete in itself, with its own characters, action, setting and style of dialogue. No cross-casting is necessary and each play could have its own director.

But this categorisation would not be quite accurate either. The three actions do have in common the present time and the sounds of warfare — gun shots, tanks and low-flying jets. This is not to say that it is sensational drama. Onstage violence does not develop beyond tears, anger and a blow on the face, together with the energy of ironic comedy and the thrust of apt and sensitive words sustained by clearly individualised speech rhythms. The strongest link between the three parts is thematic; the revelation of distinct private worlds of faith, hope and love, all fighting for existence in a world that seems unsusceptible to change.

The unconventional form of LOST WORLDS is no gimmick. It is entirely appropriate to the author's view of life today and it focuses attention progressively tighter and closer to everyone's experience. The final and most familiar of the lost worlds is presented through the performance of a Westernised Asiatic detainee, so that where sympathy is most ready and the focus most intense, no easy empathy can obliterate the challenge of the earlier two acts.

For
KAREN MENDELSOHN

CAST OF FIRST LONDON PRODUCTION

Lost Worlds was first presented by the National Theatre Company at the Cottesloe Theatre, London on 12 May 1978. The company was as follows:

Newsflash

Bella	Anna Manahan
Dot	Brenda Fricker
Frances	Philomena McDonagh
Minna	Rynagh O'Grady

Wedding Breakfast

Tom	Jon Morrison
Eina	Veronica Duffy
Rosy	Anna Manahan

Roost

Angkor	Sarah Lam
Barbara	Brenda Fricker

The play was directed by Robert Kidd

Designer: William Dudley; **Lighting:** William Dudley and Laurence Clayton; **Production Manager:** Peter Kidd; **Stage Manager:** John Caulfield; **Deputy Stage Manager:** Frank Nealon; **Assistant Stage Managers:** Pauline Asper, Jessica Barry, Angela Fairclough and Teresa Joselyn; **Sound:** David Foister; **Assistant to the Designer:** Robert Dein.

Lost Worlds

NEWSFLASH

CHARACTERS

Bella
Dot
Frances
Minna

NEWSFLASH

An isolated farmhouse overlooking a valley. The upper floor is derelict and hasn't been used for years. A heavily draped window overlooks the valley.

A winter's evening.

Bella, *an elderly woman, bedridden for years, lies propped up in bed, her eyes opening occasionally.*

Her eldest daughter **Frances** *reads to her from a Bible.*

Minna *knits.*

Dot *paces about in a bored fashion before pulling open the drapes and looking out.*

Frances *(reading):* '— Cast it on the ground. And he cast it on the ground. And it became a serpent. And Moses fled from before it —'

Dot: Saracens?

Minna: I can't hear anything.

Frances *(without looking up):* Shut the drapes.

Dot: Come and look across the valley, Minna. See — the lights of the houses are being switched on and off as a warning.

Frances: It's draughty tonight.

Dot *(closing the drapes):* Why can't we have electricity!

Frances *(shutting the Bible):* Once it was against our Faith now it's too expensive.

Dot: Isn't there something we can sell.

Frances: This is our heritage. Besides, the land is needed for the chickens and the few heads of beef.

Minna: Who's going to buy land in this troubled area.

Dot: I wish at least I had my own bedroom.

Frances: You are welcome if you can make something of the dereliction upstairs.

Dot: No thank you. I shall stay with you and Minna in the backroom. *(shuddering)* I could never go up there. It creaks like a wooden ship on a sea of woodworms.

Minna *(making a face):* Oh, Dot, we're only a small farmhouse on the side of a hill.

      Bella *stirs*

Frances: We must be peaceful for mother's sake.

Bella *(as if reining up a pony and trap):* Who has overfed the pony with corn again. He is disgracing us. Now the wheel is squealing. We are a fine travelling exhibition to all our neighbours . . . Frances!

Frances: Yes, mother.

Bella: Get off the trap and ask that good-looking fellow over there for an oilcan. Do you suppose he can fix our pony as well — Why does he walk so slowly?

Frances: He is a labourer walking on someone else's land.

Bella: Well, he won't get any at the pace he's going. Still, there's enough on his boots already to start a celery bed. *(pause)* What's he doing now?

Frances: He's looking through the toolbox of a threshing machine . . . but he's in no hurry.

Bella *(whipping up the pony):* Let's leave insolence to Heaven's Judgement! *(she closes her eyes)*

Dot: Will she ever stop driving that pony and trap!

Frances: We must keep her in good humour.

Dot: After all these years!

Frances: She is happy in her own way.

Minna: But mother is —

Frances: Mother is fine.

Bella: Everytime I look into his face I can guess what scene the first man on the moon will gaze upon — such a stoney, cratered, grey, windless landscape mixture of day and night.

Dot: She's on about father again. Leave the dead alone, mother.

Minna: We must get a doctor for her.

Frances: To mend gossamer with catsgut. They're nothing but glorified vets around here. No, we will carry on as we have always done.

Dot: Like day-old-chicks in the feathers of a wind-swept hen?

Frances: Poor mother! You are the most wicked of us all, Dot.

Minna: We shall pray for you on Sunday.

Frances: I doubt if God will want to hear her name until she has made full restitution for her remarks.

Dot *(exasperated):* I cannot live in the wilderness of the Bible anymore.

Minna *(horrified):* Dot!

Frances: Be careful! You are straying from the path.

Dot: I await here on Mount Sinai.

Frances *(quoting):* 'The lip of truth shall be established for ever, but, a lying tongue is but for a moment.'

Minna: *I* would never lie, Frances.

Bella *(opening her eyes and whipping up the pony):* The pony — He has left his morse code on the way to Crossmaglen. It is a reading of our characters . . . an S-O-S to the 'generous' soul who filled his belly to bursting. *(pause)* Keep your heads down till I pass this low-hanging branch. The last bit of money owing on the farm will be paid today to the English bank manager Ernest Littlejack. He thinks we are simple folk with cow's clap on our shoes and won't let us cross his threshold if he suspects our shoes . . . for an Englishman's home is his castle. The farm has been ours for generations . . . drunk-out almost by one or another's grandfather. Now we have made it solid . . . for an Irishman's home is his history. *(she closes her eyes)*

Dot: Will she ever get away from nineteen sixty-one!

Minna: All calendars should have been torn up after nineteen-sixty-one. I was thirteen, you were fourteen and Frances was fifteen —

Dot: That's right . . . keep reminding us.

Minna: There was scarcely a car on the road all day. The steel hoops on the wheels ground on the gravel like rock-salt on a grater. We let the pony drink from a solid slide of stream water . . . a bee was buzzing faintly as if it was coming from an old gramophone record —

Dot: One day I walked through Killeter Forest. Suddenly I came across this man and his two children. 'Excuse me,' I said, 'have you seen my husband and children. My husband is a bit older than I am. His hair is slightly grey like the foam

5

on the sea after a storm. He wears a tweed jacket with a pipe peeping from the top pocket. Our son is ten and our daughter is seven. They have curly hair and dark eyes and are always laughing. You could never fail to recognise them. Whenever we are walking, which is frequent, they love to play tricks on me by running away to hide. If you see me alone in the forest some more you will understand.'

Frances: You ARE wicked!

Minna: That is lying, Dot. *(pause)* Isn't it, Frances.

> **Frances** *looks at* **Dot** *a moment before bursting into tears and running out of the room.*

But she keeps telling ME not to lie!

Dot: It's time mother had her soup.

Minna: Was there a man with two children in Killeter Forest?

Dot: Make sure to strain the soup first.

Minna: I don't know of anyone immediately around here with two children.

Dot: The pot will be hopping off the stove if you don't hurry.
*(**Minna** goes)*

> *She pulls open the drapes and looks out but closes them quickly as* **Bella** *stirs.*

(rearranging the pillows) Sit up a bit, mother.

Bella: Is the sun decent in the sky.

Dot: It's a beautiful day, mother. Now . . . it's time for your nourishment.

Bella: We will draw into McCaffrey's Tea Rooms and get something into us. Better not mention this to your father. He's too practical a man. Always wanting to know the LSD of everything. He'd have the pony crawling to Sodom and Gomorrah on its knees tired out if he thought he could get a halfpenny off a stone of wheat flour.

Dot *(rearranging the bedclothes)*: There, there, mother —

Bella: Is that Frances?

Dot *(looking around quickly)*: Yes . . . I'm here.

Bella: You're the best and most sensible girl of the three of you.

> **Minna** *arrives quietly and unnoticed with the soup and stops to watch* **Dot**.

Dot *(taking a flower from the vase and holding it under* **Bella**'s *nose)*: Is that not lovely!

Bella: Lily of the valley. You always had good taste, Frances.

Dot *(quickly looking around and seeing* **Minna***):* Come . . . and feed her slowly. But make sure it's cool enough for a cat to eat first — What are you waiting for!

Minna: Don't be angry with me, Dot. I couldn't stand it if you were angry.

Dot: Pat her gently on the back if she chokes.

Minna: But I know that, Dot.

Bella: Sit down in the cart, Minna, before we arrive with an accident case.

Minna *(feeding her):* Yes . . . *(in tears)* mother.

Dot *(taking the spoon):* Let me feed her. You're too nervous. *(as* **Minna** *burst into tears)* Read her from the book of Exodus, chapter three.

Minna *(crying):* 'Now Moses — Moses kept the flock of Jethro his father-in-law . . . the priest of Midian. And he led the flock to the backside of the desert —'

Frances *(appearing quietly, she looks at them a moment):* Why is mother being fed so soon . . . THAT is her two-a.m. feed. *(taking the Bible)* Don't read when you are crying, Minna. The tears will stick the pages together —

Minna *(sobbing):* Yes, Frances.

Frances *(taking the bowl and spoon away from* **Dot***):* We must not waste our time walking in Killeter Forest while mother needs us so much —

Bella: Is there anything behind us, Frances?

Frances: No, mother.

Bella: Then put your hand out we're turning right. It's a treacherous stretch of the road here — 'Coffin Corner' it's called. *(pause)* Hmmpht! Look at them with their new tractor. The whole family decked out in their best. You'd be hard put to know if it was a churching, christening or croaking they were coming or going to. Don't look at them! I wouldn't please them . . . hanging on to the tractor there like winded crows on a weather cock. Hold on tight! Listen to their machine! They're like cavorting skeletons on a corrugated iron roof. *(lunging out)* There's a crack for the pony for jitterbugging with them — Let me smell that flower again, Frances.

Frances *(holding the lily of the valley under her nose):* Now promise to have a nice rest, mother.

Bella *(sniffing):* 'Return of happiness' . . . flowers have our character, Frances. *(she closes her eyes)*

Minna *(beside* **Bella***):* Do you really like the flowers that I picked for you, mother.

Frances: You will upset mother if you keep crying.

Dot: Mother likes your flowers, Minna.

Minna *(sniffing as she looks at* **Dot***):* Yes . . . she does.

> **Frances** *picks up the Bible and reads to herself.* **Minna** *continues her knitting.* **Dot** *slowly paces the room*

Frances *(glancing up):* Do you have to keep walking up and down.

Minna *(reciting):* Clap your hands and daddy will come home. Cakes in his pocket *(pointing at* **Frances***)* and you'll get none — *(she stops, embarrassed)*

Dot *(to herself):* We're the echo of a loud roar through some long forgotten battlefield.

Frances: You make me nervous walking up and down.

> *Echoing gunfire across the valley. The sisters wait petrified for it to end*

Bella: People are so silent today. There isn't a pattern, tape or rule . . . scales, four-gill-jugs nor meter that could get the shape, size or content of their thoughts.

Frances *(fearfully):* Mother, keep quiet a moment.

Bella: Is that Frances?

Frances: Yes, I'm here. *(holding her hand)* Don't trouble yourself . . . everying is all right.

Bella: If everything is all right why bother to say it?

Dot *(opening the drapes):* They're signalling again. There must be a lot of activity tonight. But I can't see anything . . . the valley is so black again.

Frances: I can't read the copy, so allow eight words.

Dot: We should move out of this area for mother's sake.

Frances: It's for mother's sake that we're here . . . this is our heritage.

Dot: This tumbledown!

Frances: It is not just a matter of clinging to a house in dilapidation but as to whether we are going to allow ourselves to be prised off the very Earth itself.

Dot: Couldn't we cling to the Earth somewhere else . . . like for example some cosy suburbia.

Frances *(angrily)*: We dwell where our forefathers' spirit lives.

Dot *(cynically)*: It is on such short black ordinary nights like these that HISTORY is made.

Frances: Snap, snap, snap at a shoal of words like a lonely pike in a flooded stone quarry.

Dot: No . . . we are fish in a tank without the sea. NOTHING can sweep us on to something better.

A creaking, grinding noise from upstairs

Minna *(looking up fearfully)*: Listen!

Frances: It's only the wind shaking the roof.

Dot *(imitating her)*: 'It's ONLY the wind shaking the roof' . . . shouldn't we look upstairs in case our heritage has suddenly sprouted wings?

Minna: Don't frighten me, Dot. You know I'm very nervous. When I was at the dentist last I passed out even though you told me that my teeth were only tiny seashells waiting to be caressed by a starfish —

Frances: Calm down, Minna.

Minna: I'm frightened, Frances. We must get out of this place. We MUST!

Frances *(to Dot)*: She's getting another of her nervous turns.

Minna *(shouting)*: I'M not, I'm NOT!

Frances: Lie down in the bedroom, Minna.

Minna: Who can help me!

Frances: I'll sit beside your bed.

Minna: It won't make any difference. I'm always alone when I feel like this —

Frances: Don't be silly!

Dot: Let her speak.

Minna: I wish you and Dot would stop arguing!

Frances: We have our differences of opinion.

Minna: Differences of opinion? I'M losing my life and for why and for what I can't remember anymore. Very soon I'll be a falling leaf.

Frances: For every falling leaf there's another one ready to join it.

Minna: THREE falling leaves amongst the nude trees! *(cynically)* Who could survive such love? Just leave me alone the both of you. Do you think I'm simple minded? *(pause)* It wasn't the gunfire in the valley or the house creaking that frightened me. It's using the last bit of beauty in this house to no good end.

> **Frances** *looks at her in puzzlement*

(indicating **Dot***)* Why is she turning her back on me? *(pulling a flower from the vase and putting it under* **Bella***'s nose)* The flowers, the flowers!

Bella: Who's there?

Minna *(eagerly):* It's Minna.

Bella: I'm not too fond of yellow chrysanthemums, Frances.

Minna *(throwing the flower on the floor):* You silly old woman! *(she runs out of the room)*

> **Frances** *and* **Dot** *look impassively at one another*

Frances: She'll be all right. How many times have we seen this sort of thing already?

Dot: Ever since she was a small girl —?

Frances: She has thrown fits of temper — You are mocking again. *(she stares vacantly at her before going to* **Bella***)*
May the Lord watch over you, mother
As the boundaries of the night
Deepen around our land
Be vigilant, dear angels of mercy
For the footprints in the sand
That betrays the agents of Lucifer.

Dot: Amen.

Frances: This is a private prayer.

Dot *(mockingly wide-eyed):* But I have always joined in before, Frances.

Frances *(looking steadily at her a moment):* You are devious.

Dot *(mock innocence):* Take that back.

Frances: I am taking sole charge of mother. You and Minna shall have to run the farm between you.

Dot *(cheerfully):* You will exhaust yourself.

Frances: Duty exhausts no one.

Dot: Oh well, if you won't let Minna and I take our turn in staying up all night with mother —

Frances *(quietly):* You don't exist for mother anymore.

Dot: I don't exist. Minna doesn't exist and you don't exist. We all ceased to exist sixteen years ago when mother first took to her bed.

Frances: I exist for mother.

Dot: Up until the age of fifteen.

Frances: It's better than nothing.

Pause

Dot: I'm getting very tired of this farm.

Frances: Then it will really go to pieces!

Dot: Let it! I've almost had enough.

Frances: We've all had a long day. *(yawning)* And I AM tired.

Dot: Mother has turned us into ghosts.

Frances: We can discuss it in the morning.

Dot: We will still be ghosts in the morning.

Frances: Daylight ghosts . . . we'll look odd, won't we.

Dot: Do you know that mother could lie there for another twenty years.

Frances *(yawning):* I feel so tired I envy her.

Dot: I will be fifty years old by then. You will be fifty-one and Minna will be forty-nine.

Frances *(to herself):* I will be fifty-one — I was just reading the other day how a woman in her fifties started to do the most amazing thing —

Dot: Birth . . . by virgin means, in some foreign country. Do you know which COUNTRY we're living in.

Frances *(startled):* That is the most appalling thing you've said today.

Dot: But it doesn't matter if we continue to live in squalor.

Frances: There is NO squalor in the Bible.

Dot *(appealing):* Frances, sell the land.

Frances *(chuckling to herself):* Sell the land.

Dot: It needn't fall cheaply *(pointing at the window)* into the wrong hands. There are overseas buyers who will pay a good price.

Frances: What will they sow — bombs . . . and will the hens sit hatching out hand-grenades? What chicks of chicanery your foreign friends would have to cluck about then?

Dot: These people can afford to let the land lie until the war is over.

Frances *(to herself):* Until the war is over? But this is only a new chapter in an old episode.

Dot: You don't believe the war will end!

Frances: I am fit and well again said the leper after he shook off a Summer cold.

Dot: Exactly what mother used to say . . . but this time we're almost destroyed.

Frances: Do *I* look as if I've almost been destroyed? *(Dot looks intently at her for a moment)* All right! *(turning her back)* Do I SOUND as if I have almost been destroyed?

Dot *(exasperated):* I render up this place . . . NOW.

Frances: Who will forgive you if you do! The generations that are dead or the generations yet to be born?

Dot *(cynically):* What a truly magnificent country we live in! Those of us alive play no significant part except as grave-diggers and midwives.

Frances *(flustered):* You are judged by mother, Minna and myself!

Dot: See this hand? It is banging the door behind me on your world.

Frances: Doors banging on people's worlds . . . next thing you'll be opening windows on the mind. True, there's a lot of work around here for a carpenter these days but very little for a philosopher.

Dot: Sell the land . . . and repair the house with part of the money.

Frances: Are you changing your trade again! I'm sorry but I could never let a philosopher make as much as a kitchen cabinet for me — the cups and saucers would argue so much all day I'd end up drinking the tea from the spout of the kettle.

Dot: With the house repaired you could stay with mother and some of the money would give Minna and I a new start . . . somewhere else.

Frances: YOU will take Minna away. What could YOU do for a Winter sapling except hoodwink the sun into thinking it's Spring.

Dot: I guarantee my plan will work.

Frances: You couldn't guarantee the next shower in a rain forest.

Dot *(furiously):* There WILL be changes!

Frances: What will you do to us? Signal to your 'friends' across the valley . . . no, I didn't mean that —

Dot: You have a lot in common with them out there tonight. They also have their dead and unborn.

Frances: Don't get caught in the middle . . . that's what I always say.

Dot: Surely you mean: 'don't appear to be in the middle'.

Frances: You might at least think of your own family.

Dot: FAMILY! Look what's left. *(pointing at* **Bella***)* An old SYCAMORE tree and her THREE Winter saplings.

Frances *(arrogantly placing her hands on her hips):* WHAT a pity we don't have an heir.

Dot: Not an heir. A child . . . that belongs to neither the graveyard nor to limbo. *(softly to herself)* A baby. But what do we know about men after all these years spent in the procreation of the farm and all its creatures . . . for the Greater Glory of — How I wish I could be knocked down on the dark grass some late evening.

Frances: I am sure you could still find someone to oblige you in Killeter Forest.

> **Dot** *sits down, hurt, and unable to answer.* **Frances** *puts her hand over her mouth and watches her*

There's no point in saying I'm sorry.

Dot *(pause):* There's no point.

Frances: Trust a dream to awaken a woman but trust a woman to awaken that dream.

> *Gunfire across the valley*

(rushing to the window and pulling open the drapes) Why can't they stop NOW!

Dot: The dead have no ears and the others haven't grown any yet.

> **Minna** *enters looking frightened*

Frances *(furiously closing the drapes):* You will NOT break up this farm. *(shaking her)* Wake up, mother.

Bella: Who's there?

Frances: Father is coming.

Minna: No please, Frances, I'm frightened.

Bella: Look at him walking towards us.

Dot: God, don't we have enough ghosts!

Bella: Take the nosebag off the pony and point his head home, Frances. We'll not get our tea and cakes at McCaffrey's now. For if we did we'd never hear the end of it. *(pause)* What did you run all those miles for, Sam? As soon as we think we're rid of you for a few hours — You're confusing to a woman, Sam. You'd have her combing her face and powdering her hair . . . if our Faith allowed it. Climb up on the cart, you're the colour of a boiled beetroot . . . running after us there like an unweaned goat. *(pause)* What's the matter? Can't you talk? Lie back on the trap and get your wind back. *(pause)* The farm is ours again, Sam, after one or another's grandfather had drunk it out — Frances, hold on to your father till I whip the pony up . . . his face has turned to curdled milk. Pull, pony, pull.

Minna *(crying out):* PULL!

Bella: Go on . . . it's only a hedgehog on the road. HURRY! My husband is dying. *(pause)* Whoa! This transport is of no further use to him. He has already made HIS journey. *(Minna cries softly)* Cover him up and stop crying. He can't be seen in his shirt sleeves or people will think we're a band of tinkers on the prowl. *(pause)* 'Now after the death of Moses the servant of the Lord *(Minna closes her eyes and prays silently)* it came to pass that Lord spake unto Joshua the son of Nun, Moses' minister saying: Moses my servant is dead, now therefore arise, go over this Jordan, thou and all this people, unto the land which I do give to them, even to the children of Israel.'

Minna: Amen.

Bella: There's no need to go to the bog-meadow for herbs, Frances . . . the cows have recovered. Why did he panic and come trekking after us for! I can't compete with Heaven now. HE's got his remedy already. All for the sake of a few poisonous plants the greedy beasts have put us all into new pastures. *(she coughs and groans)*

Minna: You're exhausting her!

Frances: There; there, mother, lie back and rest.

Bella: Imagine . . . this time a week ago I was boasting about never ailing a day in my life. Now I'm almost beyond mortal touch.

Frances: We will run the farm until you are better. I will see that Dot and Minna go to school every day.

Bella: No one must be the wiser. I'll be up again as fresh as a dawn blackbird . . . you'll see.

Frances: No one will be the wiser.

Bella: We have no man now to keep the farm safe.

Frances: WE will keep the farm safe, mother. The light of Heaven shines down on us.

    Pause.

Bella: Turn the jasmine lamp up . . . I can't see properly.

Frances: The jasmine lamp?

Bella *(exasperated):* It's on the fireboard.

Frances: I can't see it, mother.

Bella: Check that Dot hasn't taken it upstairs again — And tell your father to hurry and harness the pony.

Dot: I won't be dragged down by the past. *(she starts to go)*

Frances *(calling out loudly):* Father! Father! *(startled,* **Dot** *turns to look at her)* Bring the pony and trap to the front door.

Minna: Oh, we're going to Crossmaglen *(embarassed, she opens her mouth silently)*

Bella: Quick, don't hang around like the longest day in Winter. Where is Dot? Aren't you all ready yet?

    Dot *involuntarily steps towards her*

Minna: *I* am, mother.

Frances: I'm going upstairs to find Dot.

Bella: Isn't it marvellous what they could do with glass in those days . . . with its climbing shrub and star-shaped flowers. It's almost a pity to light it.

Frances: She was using it to pluck her eyebrows by.

Dot: YOU stopped me from going to Crossmaglen that day!

Bella: I forbid THAT in this house. We can't have the beginnings of a wild woman here.

Frances: She pulled my hair but I got the lamp, mother.

Bella: Just for that you'll stay at home and help your father with the milking.

Dot *(involuntarily):* MOTHER —!

Bella: Hurry, Frances, it's nearly dawn. *(clicking her tongue and whipping up the pony)* Lift your head and untangle your legs! (**Dot** *steps forward but retreats again)*

Frances: Drive on, mother! Dot is trying to catch us up.

Bella *(whipping):* Pony, swallow the road like a black ribbon! *(pause)* She'll need wings on her feet to catch us now.

Frances *(jeering):* Ha haaa, you'll never catch us now!

Dot *(fiercely striding forward and slapping* **Frances***):* Oh yes I can!
     Minna *screams.*

Bella: Is that her calling?
     Frances *sits down with her hand to her face.* **Minna**
     stands fearfully looking at **Bella.** **Dot** *stands petrified a*
     moment before defiantly pacing the room.
Be better brought up and give me an answer. *(pause)* I want
an answer.

Minna *(bursting into tears):* Answer her, Frances.
     Frances *ignores her*

Dot *(stopping in front of* **Bella***):* You've had your answer a long
time ago, mother. NOW look at the way we live.

Minna *(panic stricken):* Don't you talk to MY mother like that!

Dot *(looking closely at* **Bella***):* I have the strangest feeling
sometimes that you are lying there laughing at us.

Frances *(jumping to her feet):* You are a DISGRACE to our flesh
and blood!

Dot: Our blood is dammed without men and our flesh is
detained by an old woman from her bed. I've come to envy
the simplest swift as it builds its nest.

Frances: Then GO! Fly away and build your nest in the
guttering of some house in Babylon.

Minna: No, Frances, we're just tired. Everything will be better
in the daylight.

Dot: What will you do, Minna, push the sun up all by yourself?

Minna: Won't it ever rise for us again?

Frances *(to* **Dot,** *quoting):* 'Cursed be he that maketh the blind
to wander out of the way. And all the people shall say,
Amen.'

Bella: Thank you, Mr Littlejack, everything is just grand now.
We have ceased to float on the foundations on a drunkard's
promise. The farm is in the woman's line of the family again.
With hard work, hard cash and hard praying we have climbed
the hill of the World and come within whispering distance of
God.

Frances: There's your answer! We will see Mr Littlejack in the morning for a bank loan.

Minna *(excited):* Are we going to Crossmaglen—

Frances: There has been far too much melancholy in this house. The time has come for us to put our affairs into order. We have crowded down here far too long since mother was laid low. The rooms upstairs shall be re-opened. We will re-stock the farm and hire someone to do the ploughing—

> *An explosion in the distance. The sisters stand a moment listening.*

Bella: What is keeping you all . . . it is nearly dawn!

Dot: I wanted to go last time. You don't know HOW much I wanted to go on that journey to Crossmaglen. I ran and ran but the pony and trap disappeared round a bend. I sat down by a stream and cried. When I had finished I could think of nothing else but vengeance. I walked home and into the milking shed. Father was running the milk through the cooler—

Minna: But you said the cows were ill through eating poisonous plants.

Dot *(looking at her intently):* Father let out a roar and called me a whore-in-the-making when he saw my plucked eyebrows. He started to chase me. I don't know why he was so angry. I climbed a ladder to the loft. He tried to follow me but slipped and fell. He lay on the ground with his hands on his chest. I shouted down to him that mother told me that she was going to ask Mr Littlejack to find her a good client to buy the farm. He got up and shouted something about near killing himself for sixteen years to build the farm . . . then he ran out of the barn crying. I didn't like what he had said about my eyebrows . . . something inside me fell apart like a dying tulip. Only my ghost was left to send him to his death along the road to Crossmaglen—

> *A loud high-pitched whistle followed by a loud explosion. The lights go out. When the lights come up again the sisters are lying on the floor with traces of blood on their faces.*

Bella: Hurry up! Well, just don't stand there, Dot. Come on . . . climb up on the trap. We are off to Crossmaglen.

The sisters rise slowly and climb on to the bed with **Bella**

(clicking her tongue and whipping) Go on, pony, set the road on fire!

(girlish laughter) Crossmaglen, Crossmaglen . . . we're on the road to Crossmaglen. *(music plays)*

Voice of Newscaster: *(music off)* — We interrupt this programme of early morning music to bring you a newsflash: An elderly woman and her three daughters were killed *(Blackout)* just before dawn today, near Crossmaglen, when a mortar bomb ripped through the roof of their isolated farmhouse during a clash between the Security Forces and armed raiders. That is the end of this newsflash. We hope to bring you more details later — Bringing the time up to five and a half minutes past eight-o-clock. *(pop music plays)*

Lost Worlds

WEDDING BREAKFAST

CHARACTERS

Tom
Eina
Rosy

WEDDING BREAKFAST

A room in a derelict house which has been hastily tidied up for the wedding breakfast.

A few chairs, a table covered by a white cloth on which there is a wedding cake, a china tea set, bottles of wine and glasses, a vase of flowers, some unlit candles and a bottle of champagne in a plastic bucket.

A window is blocked up. Light comes from a camping calor-gas lamp.

A doorway leading to the interior of the house has been blocked up with concrete blocks but a hole has been knocked through the blocks to allow people to enter. Against this hole is an old door shored-up with a piece of timber.

Tom *and* **Eina,** *a teenage couple have just been married.* **Eina** *wears her short, white wedding dress and* **Tom** *a dark suit. They sit silently holding hands and watch* **Rosy,** *an older woman, arrange the wedding table.*

Eina: Do you think they'll know where to come, Tom?

Tom: Was everyone told, Rosy?

Rosy *(indicating table):* It's been ONE job getting everything here . . . I hope they do.

Eina *(listening):* Our wedding bells are still ringing for us and we're here already.

Tom: We were lucky to get through that roadblock. *(Eina kisses him on the cheek)* I wonder how long I can risk staying here.

Eina: TOM . . . we've only just been married.

Rosy: You're best to wait till dark as arranged.

Eina *(kissing him):* My darling, we're together for ever now.

Rosy *(glancing at her a moment):* Don't get too lovable, Eina, you might be climbing the back yard wall yet . . . wedding dress or no wedding dress, if we're raided.

Tom: I hope we're safe enough here, Rosy.

Rosy *(angrily):* One derelict house is much the same as another in this silent street of wreck and ruin.

Tom: You tidied up well, Rosy.

Rosy *(softening):* It's the least I can do as a neighbour — *(outburst)* Oh, I told you to stop throwing stones at the Authorities when you were a wee boy! Now look at you — a young man, NUMBER ONE on the hit-and-run-parade . . . hope you're proud of yourself. *(wiping a tear from her eye)* Your mother couldn't even be at the wedding in case she was followed.

Tom *(putting his arm around her):* I'm going to be out of the country soon . . . and when I'm settled I'll send for Eina —

Eina: You never told me that, Tom.

Tom *(winking at her. To* **Rosy***):* You can come and visit us — *(hugging her)* And mother as well.

Eina *(appealingly):* Tom. *(he kisses her)* What IS going to happen?

Tom: Let's think about our wedding breakfast.

Eina: I was thinking about mammy and daddy and my sisters . . . and how they couldn't be at our wedding either.

Tom: Let's think about US now.

Eina *(looking around her):* Look at this terrible place. It's cold as well.

Tom: That's funny . . . I feel the opposite.

Eina *(exasperated):* Oh . . . you're stupid!

Tom *(holding her close):* Feeling warmer?

Rosy *(whispering):* Shoo, a moment! *(listening)* I thought I heard a car.

> **Tom** *quickly puts his hand inside his jacket and slowly draws his empty hand out*

That's one habit you'll have to forget for now.

Tom *(angrily looking at his hands):* Where's the protection! I feel like a dozen eggs in a car-breaker's yard.

Rosy: You can't risk a shooting at a time like this, Tom.

Tom: I must have been MAD to listen to you, Rosy.

Rosy: You've got a young wife now . . . never mind me being with you here.

Tom: I won't go down without a struggle.

Rosy: Give your head an hour's peace on your wedding day.

Tom: Tell *them* outside to give me peace!

Eina: Tom . . . don't argue so much.

Tom: I couldn't argue with you, my sweetheart.

> **Eina,** *disappointed, turns her back on him*

What's the matter . . . my wee honey-bee?

Eina: Oh, don't call me that name!

Tom: But you always liked it before.

Eina: Well, I don't like it now.

Rosy *(looking at them a moment):* Look, I'm going out to check-up with our look-outs.

Tom: Give three bangs when you get back.

> *He removes the timber. Before crouching down, in order to get through the hole,* **Rosy** *turns and smiles at them*

(replacing the timber) I don't know where we would be without her.

Eina *(after a pause):* Wouldn't it be nice to be at my mammy's home . . . the fire roaring, the neighbours dropping in for a drink and a mouthful to eat, to wish us well, unwrapping the presents . . . waiting for the car to come and take us on our honeymoon — *(she stops apologetically)*

Tom: The struggle goes on —

Eina *(vaguely):* What?

Tom: We'll grow stronger until there's *no* place safe for them.

Eina: Oh!

Tom: I wish I'd done all they claimed I'd done.

Eina: Can't I come with you.

Tom: I'm not sure where I'll be hiding out yet.

Eina: Will you write to me.

Tom: Of course I will.

Eina *(excited):* I'll wait for the postman every day!

Tom: You'll get my letters by courier.

Eina *(disappointed):* All right.

Tom: It's the only way to avoid the post office censor.

Eina: You are going to write me love letters?

Tom: Lots of them.

23

Eina: Why did you tell Rosy that you were leaving the country?

Tom: I wanted to give her some hope.

Eina: What about some hope for me!

Tom: Rosy's generation liked to talk about doing something about our life in the old days. Now that WE'RE doing it she doesn't want to believe it — Anything to keep her happy.

Eina *(holding him):* I'M happy, Tom.

Tom *(misunderstanding):* Because YOU understand what the war is all about.

Eina: Let's not talk about it now.

Tom *(drawing her close):* We'll put it right out of our minds.

Eina: I wish our guests would arrive —

Tom *(whispering):* Just a moment.

> *They listen as a number of vehicles slowly pass up the street.*
>
> *Three bangs. They stand still a moment before* **Tom** *lets* **Rosy** *in*

Rosy *(breathlessly):* Armoured convoy . . . there might be a search.

Tom: Did you see anybody —?

Rosy: The look-outs will hold their positions — Oh, Frank won't be here . . . he's had to dive for cover himself.

Tom: Let's begin the wedding breakfast.

Rosy: If you want, Tom.

Eina: NO, Tom, let's wait a bit longer.

Tom: I should have got out of the area sooner —

Eina: I'm glad we got married in OUR church.

Tom *(nodding):* But what a risk.

Eina: It's worth it on the best day of our lives.

Tom: We'll show them that they can't get us down. *(turning on the transistor)* Let's dance.

Rosy *(moving awkwardly):* What's it called?

Eina: 'The Signalman' — look, put your arms like this . . . your left foot here . . . wait for the first bar of the music . . . RIGHT . . . that's IT . . . orange for caution . . . slow down . . . red to stop . . . get ready to move . . . orange-red . . . s-l-o-w-l-y . . . move . . . green to go — That's it! You're not doing bad—

Rosy *(whooping):* UUUU HOOOO!

Eina: You've gone old-fashioned again, Rosy. LOOK! Like this.
> **Tom** *stops dancing and looks at them.*

What's the matter, my love? *(he looks at them without answering)*

Rosy: Thinking about something.
> *He stands listening to the music*

Eina *(turning off the transistor):* What is it, Tom?

Tom *(looking around the room):* The shape of this room . . . this shelf. I remember a similar one somewhere. *(crouching)* I was able to stand under it. My hair barely touched the underside.

Rosy *(teasing):* You've grown.

Eina: Mrs Levine once lived here.

Rosy: Don't YOU remember that, Tom!

Eina: She was caught in crossfire —

Tom: Had a son called Matthew. When I was five —

Eina: Booby-trapped car —

Tom *(dreamingly):* What.

Eina: A year ago. He was passing this parked car —

Tom: Jimmy —

Rosy: The father . . . a great man for the dogs.

Eina: Found in a river bound and gagged.

Rosy *(tutting):* Tragic . . . lightning strikes twice and three times in the same spot in this country.

Tom *(lost in thought):* Matthew . . . fourteen years ago —
No, couldn't have been this house.

Rosy: This is only ONE house lost now in two dead streets . . . bombed-out, blazed-out — concrete blocks for doors and windows . . . on the edge of the 'Peace-Line'.

Eina: How DID we ever manage in the old days before the peace-line.

Rosy: Usually between 'them' and 'us' you'd have two or three families that were neutral.

Eina *(laughing):* Neutral! Which side were they neutral on?

Rosy: I was neutral once.

Eina *(in wonderment):* How did you manage that!

Rosy: 'Isn't this a lovely morning, that's a grand evening, a red sky at night is the shepherd's delight, a taste of rain in the air —'

Tom: Nineteen sixty-three —

Rosy: You were both five . . . Matthew and you.

Tom: Biggest worry then was where the next bag of potato crisps were coming from —

Eina: Spudniks!

Tom *(lost in thought again):* Spudniks . . .

Eina: I liked that brand of potato crisps.

Tom *(pointing):* Right there was an old sofa with a gash in it. I put my hand in once and found ten pence. Mary allowed me to put it in my pocket even though she didn't usually have enough money —

Rosy: Mary! That was the poor woman's name. We all called her Mrs Levine because she kept herself to herself a lot . . . it's amazing how we can forget names.

Tom: Matthew had a pal called Dessie —

Rosy *(quickly):* Dessie Roche —

Eina: He's doing 'Life'.

Tom *(irritated):* I know that! I was trying to remember further back.

Rosy: He was a nice wee fellow . . . when he was young.

> **Tom** *turns his back on her.*

(quickly) This street was right and lively then. All the doors were open till eleven-o'clock at night. No blinds on the windows. The children could hop from one pool of light to another . . . right all the way up the street. The corner shop was open till midnight and would be open again at five in the morning to sell, hot fresh O'Hara baps.

Eina: What about the fish-and-chip shop that sold home-made ice-cream, honeycomb and fudge.

Rosy: Mario Fuento . . . awful nice man.

Eina: Machine-gunned from a car three years ago.

Rosy: I loved wee Sophia . . . wasn't she lovely with her black ringlets and dark brown eyes —

Eina: Her mother —

Tom *(quickly):* Took her back to Italy.

Eina *(with a sigh of relief):* To Tuscany.

Rosy: That place sounds nice.

Tom *(picking up a bottle from the table):* Now it's champagne!

Rosy: Something I used to only see in the Greta Garbo films.

Eina: Don't open it yet, Tom.

Tom *(loudly)*: It's supposed to go *(loudly)* POP!

Eina *(softly):* Not so loud.

Tom *(looking at the food):* I feel hungry.

Eina: Don't touch anything, Tom.

Tom *(glancing at her):* Hurry them up, Rosy.

Rosy: Look, Eina, I'll just have another wee look around.

Eina: Don't bother yourself, Rosy . . . I'm sure they'll be here soon.

Tom: FOUR knocks this time, Rosy . . . when you get back.

> **Eina** *shakes her head at* **Rosy**

Rosy *(to* **Eina***):* You may not be together for a long time. *(she goes)*

> **Tom** *looks at* **Eina** *a moment before going to her*

Eina *(retreating slightly):* Do you suppose one of our presents might be an electric toaster.

Tom *(advancing):* Or a four-foot, blue fluorescent teddy bear.

Eina *(retreating):* Maybe a cuckoo clock with a weather man and a weather woman —

Tom *(advancing):* Divided by a 'peace line'.

Eina *(retreating):* God, we'd need one in here!

Tom *(stopping):* What's the matter, my wee honey bee.

Eina: I want things to be done properly.

Tom: I'm facing 'Life' if the assassination squads don't get me first.

Eina: A woman always remembers the first time.

Tom: No matter who?

Eina *(quietly):* If she loves him.

Tom *(after a pause):* Remember that old film 'For Whom The Bell Tolls'?

Eina: At the club . . . two weeks ago.

Tom: With Ingrid Bergman and Cary Grant —

Eina: No . . . with Ingrid Bergman and GARY COOPER.

Tom: Isn't it funny . . . getting the dead mixed-up with the living.

Eina: No . . . it's not 'funny'.

Tom: I didn't mean that sort of 'funny'. *(he turns away from her and kicks the wall)*

Eina: What were you going to say, Tom.

Tom: It doesn't seem important now.

Eina *(appealing):* Oh, Tom, tell me.

> *Pause*

Tom: They shared a sleeping bag outside the cave, beside the fire . . . Ingrid Bergman and Cary — *(banging the wall)* GARY — FUCKING — COOPER —! It's all spoilt now.

Eina *(softly):* Not between us, Tom.

Tom: I hope not.

Eina: Tom . . . you're not sorry you married me!

Tom *(in a low voice):* No.

Eina *(scolding):* Say it with meaning.

Tom *(loudly):* NO . . . NO . . . NO! I'm not sorry I married you. *(softly)* I'm not sorry.

Eina: I believe you.

Tom *(tightening his arms around her):* I long for you. I —

Eina *(breaking free. Listening):* What was that!

Tom *(in despair):* Oh, my God, not again!

Eina: I DO hear something.

Tom *(disbelieving):* Outside or inside.

Eina: Somewhere inside.

Tom: Maybe it's our guests coming through the holes in the dividing walls further down the street.

Eina: Couldn't we have found a 'safe house' for our wedding breakfast at least.

Tom: What house! I can't even get out of the area. It's sealed. Now they're moving in. It's only a matter of time till they get HERE.

Eina *(sudden moment of panic):* What'll we do!

Tom: The OLD strategy . . . wait till they have searched a street then nip in there.

> **Eina** *puts her hand to her head in a moment of despair*

Don't worry, my sweatheart, we'll soon be in some friendly house watching them search for me on television . . . just after the cartoons come on.

Eina *(fearfully):* Then what?

Tom: Then it's MAN into GHOST!

Eina: Take me with you.

Tom: We've gone over this before, Eina.

Eina: I'll take a chance.

Tom: It's too dangerous.

Eina: No one will ever notice a couple in love.

Tom: It's every couple in love they're after now. Besides, they've probably examined the church register already.

Eina: Wouldn't it be nice if Rosy came back with a broomstick. We'd get on it . . . *(looking at the ceiling and breathing deeply)* and FLY away!

Tom: After we dive-bombed the BASTARDS!

Eina: NO!

Tom *(holding her):* People tell me what I'm doing is right . . . and if I'm not right there's nothing I can do now. So, everything in my life must become a weapon NOW. *(pointing at the table)* The knives, the forks, the bottles . . . even OUR wedding cake is big enough to hide a five-pound-bomb inside. My head is full of wiring circuits and escape routes. *(pause)* What else can I do but fight. My grave was bought before I was born.

Eina *(startled):* Oooh! *(recovering, she stands perfectly still)*

Tom: Right now an eight-year-old boy is throwing a stone at a saracen and an old granda is patting him on the head. *(thinking)* Maybe that's the way it should be . . . the generations together again for once in fifty years.

Eina *(firmly):* We must eat something.

Tom: You're right, my honey bee . . . let's eat.

      Church bells ring out

Eina: Teresa's married! *(whooping)* Teresa and Frank!

Tom *(opening a bottle of spirits):* Let's drink to them. *(pouring)* Good health, Frank and Teresa!

Eina *(joyously raising her glass):* GOOD LUCK! GOOD LUCK! GOOD LUCK! . . . Teresa and Frank! *(dancing around)* That IS marvellous! Have a gorgeous time, Teresa and Frank.

Tom: He just got out a few days ago.

Eina *(vaguely):* Who?

Tom: Frank.

Eina: Are you sure?

Tom: He was in the 'Kesh' . . . 'the Lazy K.'

Eina: Isn't there just ONE person not mixed up in anything?

Tom *(thinking):* Liberace? *(she turns her back)* Oh, I'm only joking. Come on, Eina, this is OUR day. *(she keeps her back* *turned)* Well, you knew me when I was part of nothing.

Eina *(turning. Sharply):* When you were seven. *(she looks at him a moment before laughing)* Spudniks . . . you gave me a bag of spudniks.

Tom: 'Donkey Head' — *(Eina is about to say something but changes her mind)* Yes, I know — he's up in the cemetery.

Eina: *I* didn't spoil everything this time, Tom.

Tom *(thinking):* He broke into the corner shop once and stole a whole carton. Then he hands them around to implicate everybody.

Eina: Maybe he was just being generous.

Tom: How often do children give you things they want themselves.

Eina: Is that why you gave that packet to me?

Tom: Yes.

Eina: But you could have given it to Teresa.

Tom: Yes.

Eina: But you didn't —

Two shots ring out in the distance

What was that?

Tom: The three-two-five converted Frisko —

She lets out a sign of exasperation

One of OUR'S. *(thinking)* Wild ginger hair like tangled brambles. He even smelt like a man then. We played 'bogeyman.' Once, it was his turn to hide in the dark alleyways while we ran past shouting: 'THE BOGEYMAN IS COMING! THE BOGEYMAN IS COMING!' It was one in the morning and pitch black because the street lamps were smashed. *I* organised the gang. Instead of us running past in a bunch I sent out a scout first — *(quickly)* I forget his name. We had a left flank and a right flank . . . and I headed the rearguard. Our scout ran past . . . nothing happened. I gave instructions for the left flank to move, covered by our rearguard . . . nothing happened. Then the right moved . . . we waited, and then we moved. I was the last 'man' in the rearguard. I had passed all the alleyways and was about to run into the light — Something dropped on me from a yard wall. I must have blacked-out. When I came round 'Donkey Head' was sitting on my chest smoking a cigarette.

Eina: He introduced us with that bag of spudniks.

Tom: I'll put some more flowers on his grave . . . first chance I get.

Eina: Don't go near the cemetery . . . it's the one place they're watching. They know that the dead have more friends than the living.

Tom: I've been to his grave more times than I've been to his house — *(he looks at her a moment)*

Eina *(gently):* I'll bring him a bunch of red roses.

Tom: And tell him 'thanks' from me.

Eina: I'll tell him 'thanks' from us.

Tom: Let's eat.

Eina: In fifteen minutes time . . . whether they arrive or not.

> *Four knocks. Startled,* **Eina** *clings to him. He removes the makeshift door and* **Rosy** *enters and stands silently*

Eina: What is it, Rosy?

Rosy: 'Crabbie' was killed.

Eina: The old one-armed paperseller . . . are you sure!

Rosy: Not five minutes ago.

Eina: But HE'S been around a long time!

Rosy: Sixty years. He was selling newspapers as a child when I was a child.

Eina *(to herself):* Those two shots.

Rosy: From a passing car.

Eina *(sitting down):* That's sickening.

Rosy: He was the only thing that never changed in this city. People came back from abroad, after years, and often remarked about the old papersellers . . . still there like Queen Victoria's statue outside the City Hall.

Tom *(grunting):* Hmpth!

Eina *(looking at him a moment):* Haven't you anything to say about it, Tom.

Tom *(thinking):* They waited till the Army had cut a swathe through the area and then followed them in quickly and then out before the re-sealing. *(scratching his head)* But how did THEY get the NEW rifle!

Rosy: Crabbie was a true friend of the neighbourhood.

> **Tom** *remains silent, lost in thought*

Eina *(looking at him a moment):* When I was five I had this doll with a sailor suit. I called him Toby. I was playing 'mothers' with Geraldine. She wanted to wash and dress him and put him to bed. But it was MY dolly . . . I brought him up. She started to argue. I held Toby tight. She was pulling my hair. But I wouldn't let him go. She grabbed hard and Toby's arm came away in her hand. I cried . . . not loud. More like a saucepan of milk boiling over. The tears fell on this thin, cotton dress I was wearing and soaked through to my chest. They were hot. I ran out of the house and up the street and bumped into Crabbie. 'Toby is hurt! TOBY IS HURT!' He picked him up and looked at him . . . and waved the bit of arm that was left in his sleeve. 'I've got a son. At LONG last I've got a son!' And he kissed Toby on the forehead.

She looks at **Tom**, *he doesn't respond.*

Rosy: There will NEVER be the like of Crabbie again.

Eina *(outburst to* **Tom***):* Don't you care about the poor man!

Tom: Why do you think they called him 'Crabbie' for . . . bad-tempered old bugger.

Rosy: That's shameful talk and the man dead.

Eina: EVERYBODY trusted him!

Tom: They will now.

Eina: Ooooh! You're heartless!

Tom: Besides, it's not a problem of trust anymore. It's a question of logic.

Eina: Who told YOU that?

Tom: Nobody TELLS you things like that.

Rosy: THEY killed him!

Tom: Yes . . . but WHY. To draw us out of our holes while the search is going on. We're not all hysterical you know.

Rosy *(looking at him a moment):* You're only a kid . . . still shitting yellow.

Tom: Maybe, but I'm not innocent anymore.

Rosy: I never thought things would come to THIS.

Tom: The same old excuse — 'when I was shouting into the night, all those years ago, it wasn't a war cry. I was only calling the cat in for his supper.'

Eina: TOM!

Rosy: The ugly duckling has grown into an ugly duck.

Tom: When hens hatch out duck eggs they're left standing on the river bank.

Rosy: I regret it all.

Tom *(after a pause):* We're going to celebrate in ten minutes time whether people arrive or not.

Rosy: It's the search . . .

Eina *(resigned):* Nobody's coming.

Rosy: They want to but everything that moves is followed. I went a mile out of my way to get back this time.

Tom: That's it! I'm not hungry anymore.

Eina: Will you be in ten minutes time?

Tom: The celebrations have ended.

Eina *(firmly):* NO.

Tom: Rosy, bring Eina back to her parent's house.

Eina: I'm not going till the last moment.

Tom: I have to try and stay here till dark.

Eina: I don't mind.

Tom: I might have to make a run for it any minute.

Eina: I'll wait until the last bitter second.

Tom: How will I think in an emergency if you stay here, Eina.

Rosy: One of our look-outs has had to change his position.

Tom: To where!

Rosy: 'Burnt' McMullen's.

Tom: Go home NOW, honey-bee, before they pick you up.

Eina: I'll be questioned anyway.

Rosy: I know . . . but at least you'll have time to change out of your wedding dress.

Eina: I WON'T change until dark.

Tom: Go on, Rosy, take her away.

Rosy *(putting her arm around her shoulders):* Come on, love.

Eina *(shaking her off):* I'm not going.

> Rosy *shakes her head and looks at* **Tom.**

Tom: You're making things dangerous for Rosy.

Rosy: Don't worry about me, Tom.

> A *machine-gun burst nearby.*

Tom *(sharply):* GO, Rosy!

> She approaches **Eina** but **Eina** clings tightly to **Tom.**
> *(trying to break free)* Away . . . QUICK, Rosy!

Rosy *(taking off her coat):* Here, Eina, wrap yourself up warm.

Eina *(still clinging to* **Tom***):* This is my wedding day.

Tom: Good luck, Rosy . . . thanks for everything. *(she goes)*
He shakes off **Eina** *and slowly paces up and down, thinking. She watches him.*

Eina: We could still celebrate.
He shakes his head and continues pacing.

Tom *(to himself):* 'Burnt' McMullens . . . bad logistics.
The sound of hammering.
The look-outs are no good to us now. We should have moved sooner.

Eina: We're trapped.

Tom: Crabbie got himself killed at a bad time.

Eina: It's my fault —

Tom: Rosy was too busy telling us —
The hammering grows louder.

Eina: What's that noise!

Tom: They're coming through the walls with sledgehammers in case of booby-traps.

Eina: I'm still glad I'm with you, Tom.

Tom: See what I mean about logic now? *(she nods her head. He removes the makeshift door)* Help me with the table. *(She looks at him)* Come on . . . QUICK!

Eina: Ask me nicely, Tom.
The hammering starts again

Tom *(kissing her quickly):* Take one end . . . hurry. *(pointing to the gap in the wall)* They're coming from that direction. *(he kisses her quickly again)*

Eina: Two baby kisses . . . and an I-O-U?

Tom: Yes, honey-bee — Now . . . LIFT!
They carry the table to the gap in the wall.

Eina: What's the idea of —

Tom: Not too near the hole . . . leave a four-foot gap. *(looking at his watch)* Good . . . it's near dusk. *(lighting the candles on the table)* When they break through to here they'll see — What?

Eina: OUR wedding breakfast.

Tom: In a derelict house in a derelict street.

Eina: They'll think the worst.

Tom: A bizarre sight.

Eina *(quietly):* The house is booby-trapped.

Tom: They'll withdraw quicker than a Trappist monk from a disco. That'll give us time to get over the back yard wall into the next street — *(as she lifts a sandwich)* NO! don't touch ANYTHING! *(tidying the table)* The neater the stranger.

Eina: Not even the champagne!

Tom: No . . . it's a lovely touch to everything.

> *The hammering stops*

Eina: Tom —

Tom *(whispering):* We must be quiet when the hammering stops. *(listening)* They are listening as well.

> *He turns off the calor-gas lamp. They stand silently until the hammering begins again.*

Eina: I'll wrap Toby up warm when I get home.

Tom: There's no time for childhood stories anymore.

Eina: But I've ALWAYS looked after Toby.

Tom *(looking at her a moment before kissing her gently):* Yes, my sweetheart.

Eina: Wasn't it nice earlier —

> *The hammering stops.*

Tom *(whispering as he looks at his watch):* Blacken your face and hands —

Eina: Ooooh!

> *He quickly puts his hand over her mouth before picking up some dirt from the floor and blackening his face and hands. She watches him.*

Tom *(whispering):* Quick!

> *She slowly picks up the dirt and blackens her face and hands.*

(holding **Rosy's** *coat)* Put this on or your wedding dress will shine in the dark.

> *He pulls her to one side of the hole as the hammering begins again.*

Eina: Wasn't it exciting . . . during the first hour . . . when we were married . . . waiting for our guests to arrive . . . guessing —

> *The hammering stops. CHURCH BELLS RING OUT. They stand silently, listening.*

BLACKOUT.

Lost Worlds

ROOST

CHARACTERS

Angkor
Barbara

ROOST

A well-lit room in a detention centre. A plain table with two chairs. On the table, a large vase of mixed flowers.

Angkor, *a young Cambodian girl sits very still, looking straight ahead. She is being detained pending the Home Secretary's decision on her deportation.*

On the other chair sits **Barbara,** *a social worker, who is endeavouring to gather sufficient medical evidence that would stop her deportation.*

Barbara: Angkor, do you know where you are? *(pause)* This is a detention centre . . . do you understand what that means? *(pause)* My name is Barbara. I am your friend. *(pause)* I do NOT work for the detention centre . . . it is important that you answer me. *(pause)* Your defence counsel has asked me to get the answer to some questions that might help to reverse the Court's recommendation that you be deported. *(pause)* You do not want to be deported, do you! *(pause)* Angkor, this is the third day that I have been trying to get through to you. Time is running out.
You are being held in custody pending the Home Secretary's decision. Angkor, do you know where you are?

> *She repeats the above speech in a low voice as* **Angkor** *rises*

Angkor: Barbara IS trying to be my friend. She is trying to help me . . . as everyone is trying to help me. But I cannot make up my mind whether I want to stay in this country or be deported. If I stay here I might be kept in detention for how long I do not know. People similar to Barbara will keep asking me questions and writing out reports, *(glancing)* as Barbara is doing now. But they can never understand how I feel. So much already has been written on yellow government paper with mysterious code numbers on the left hand side. I do not think such paper will ever be allowed to bear the marks of how I truly feel. Yet, if I am deported I am going back to a country that I may not recognise anymore.

She sits down and resumes her former posture

Barbara: Angkor, tell me what is going through your head right now. What made you injure your foster-parents.

Startled, **Angkor** *puts her hand to her head*

(excitedly) Can you hear me!

Angkor . . . answer me. What made you injure your foster-parents. They are in hospital.

She repeats the above speech a number of times in a low voice

Angkor *(rising):* It was a beautiful Sunday morning. The sun was shining. Sophie and William my foster-parents were sitting in the patio. The weather was SO lovely. I called them Sophie and William because some kids at my college had started to call THEIR parents by their first names. Sophie was upset. William called it 'a trend'. It wasn't that William was unkind. He was a very generous man . . . that is, he found it easier to give presents than to give anything else. I think he got more afraid of me as I started to grow into a young woman. I was startled when he gave me a skateboard for my birthday. Sophie, who understood me better, gave me some very expensive perfume. I played with the skateboard . . . why not, it was fun. That morning I was in the patio practising 'knee-dips' and 'whoop-tee-doodles.' William and Sophie were having an argument. I think it was about me. Had I become 'introverted'? Did I 'lack communication'? I was almost sure they were referring to me. Each time I came near them on the board they would pull on a smile that seemed too tight for their faces. I 'rode at anchor' and studied them. Sophie in particular was very anxious about something this morning. She was very quiet about it. When William was anxious he would rationalise it into a big speech. He was a real paper-dragon. He could be set on fire by the three serious 'Sundays' and their magazines. It was an all-day battle for him, shouting: 'My God, Sophie, come and look SCARFE has done it again!' Then he would go into his BIG speech. *I* was his Third World. He would clear his throat and Sophie would be quiet:

'I sometimes think that all this reading of the Sundays only emphasises our torpidity. Here we have condensed reports from all over the world which seem to be saying *(banging the table)* ACT! Do something . . . NOW! . . . about these social disgraces. Once more we dutifully car-wash our consciences . . . our loathing for injustice is stirred, our sexual desires inflamed and our fighting spirits sharpened —! But what are we but citizens of a-five-grain-valium-republic . . . subjects of a monochrome monarchy.'

He always read the business sections last. These, he said, were the more realistic . . . no propaganda, no colouring, no personal viewpoints — the only section of the paper where the capitalists doubted their own beliefs each Sunday. I hadn't the heart to tell him that it takes ONE to know ONE. Sometimes he called me 'little comrade' which I loathed. Things were so trendy in our area that if one was to throw a stone one was bound to hit a marxist. He even called Sophie a bourgeois bitch once because she had forgotten to order his 'Southern Comfort.'

It was so pleasant that Sunday. The lame-looking, rusty geriatric tree had blossomed . . . the fragrant fingers of the magnolia blossoms pointed to the blue silk sky. Not a cloud in sight. What a pity I feel so restless today. I wandered indoors and fiddled with the radio hoping to find a good sound. Once, while listening to the shortwave bands *(children's voices singing an Asian song)* I swear I heard my language. Sophie was certain I had forgotten my language. She was very upset and said I was incoherent in ANY language when we first met. I tried the shortwave again — the sound of sausages frying . . . a giant yodelling in space . . . and then music — I SWEAR, I SWEAR it is familiar to me! I turned it up loud lest it would fade. Where had I heard it before? I couldn't remember. It started to fade — I TRIED and TRIED to bring it back but only a mournful Arab song answered me.

When I returned to the patio I knew that William and Sophie were once more wondering what I had been up to. William, who dashes in where angels, etc., asked me did I have strong tastes in music besides Berlioz . . . meaning, of course, did I like Asian music. Yes I did but — No, I was not listening to 'THE EAST IS RED' . . . yes, of course, I know it is Chinese, isn't it? Once it was played on the 'Fun Thirty' by — No, I was listening to something that sounded familiar. No, it had never been played by any local radio station. How was it familiar? I don't know that yet. Sophie was silent because she agreed with William interrogating me. Usually she would make him into a loud braying ass just by giving him one of her surgical looks. She is a doctor with that cleansing look that can render the dust beneath her feet free from bacteria. I couldn't understand what they were so worried about. William wanted to drop the whole matter to some future date. That was William — 'don't do today what you will never do tomorrow.' Well . . . that is what Sophie said of him. His architectural company made a fortune out of high-rise blocks . . . for housing. A short distance from here William once chained himself to an antique pillar-box that was under threat by the Post Office. That is William . . . Sophie told me: 'He ALWAYS saw the trees for their wood.' He was sitting there drinking his malt beer and complaining that this interruption by Sophie was putting him at least two magazines and an arts review behind. But his little brain with its own independent power supply was working somewhere inside that three-tier head of his . . . yes, I'm afraid Sophie said that as well.

Pop music. **Angkor** *sits down*

Barbara: Angkor, why did you injure William and Sophie . . . I know you liked to call them that. *(pause)* What are you reasoning out inside that pretty head of yours? Shall I write down that you are maliciously refusing to co-operate — *(sighing)* If only I could have some rational explanation that some of our old magistrates could understand. *(pause)* I have contacted the Petrilli Trust responsible for bringing children like you from less developed countries. The problem is that they don't even know what your real name is. You were found in a refugee camp near the Vietnam border with Cambodia. That is all we know. Under the terms of the Petrilli Trust you were supposed to be brought here for training and education only and then to be returned to your country of origin. You signed this agreement when you were nine years old — Of course, we are questioning the legality of asking nine year olds to sign such an agreement. Then William and Sophie sponsored you and became your foster-parents. Now they are very ill in hospital, but, the indications are that they never want to see you again. *(pause)* You see, Angkor, they are terrified of you now and very sadly disappointed. As I see it the Petrilli Trust agreement will be invoked.

Won't you let me help you? Try to think back to that day when William and Sophie were so badly injured by shooting. What led up to it?

She repeats the last speech repeatedly in a low voice as **Angkor** *rises to her feet.*

Angkor: It was such a beautiful day but I was still restless. Sophie and William were relaxing. But they made it seem more like lethargy. *(pop music)* Now William was complaining about the record being too loud. He couldn't concentrate on 'Lifespan' which was explaining how to 'BUDGET WITH WARTIME COOKING.' Sophie was angry with him and told him to stop reading comic-cuts. William quite logically said that adults sometimes needed comic-cuts. Sophie apologised and said that was true. She winked at me in order to make me part of her female conspiracy.

The phone was ringing from within the house. We sat in the patio looking at one another. It was probably Melanie. She and I usually had a walk on Sundays . . . and stopped off for an iced drink or a coffee at FARQUHARSONS. It was there, with a lot of blinking, that we smoked a cigarette. It wasn't that I was forbidden to smoke — William and Sophie were too progressive to forbid ANYTHING. I didn't want to disappoint them by smoking in front of them. They had given it up such a long time ago that when we had guests no one could ever remember where the ashtrays had been put. I asked Sophie to give my apologies to Melanie when she answered the phone. It was she who usually answered when none of us moved. When she was gone William gave me a look that said: 'Come on, out with it, what is it!' But what he said was something entirely different: 'Your mother is

43

nervous this morning. How can we help her?' Then, in his awkwardness, he turned to one of the magazines: 'PEANUTS is very funny this week —' Then he clasps it to his breast like one will do when playing with a five-year-old: 'But you can't have it! I am reading RUDIMENTS OF WISDOM. Did you know there are such things as ice-worms. There are actually worms in the Polar ice . . . millions upon millions of them. Bring them up to room temperature and they die. Isn't that FASCINATING! It all started with the discovery by the Monk —'

Sophie was back and looked at us a moment . . . wondering why her re-appearance had caused this abrupt silence. William looked guiltily at her for no reason I could understand. All *I* could do was beam upon her which seemed to make her contort her body in a sudden movement of anger. 'Why can't you answer the phone when you know it is going to be your friend Melanie!' Sophie is not usually as directly angry to me. When we are in the patio she will complain to the birds in the magnolia tree. Indoors she makes a loud banging in the kitchen.

The sun is really hot now. William is reminded of his National Service days in the Malay Peninsula. He smiles at me when he says this. I expect *I* remind him of the Malay Peninsula and not the sun. I wonder if he had a love affair there. Being a brilliant young man — on his own admission — he had been seconded to military intelligence to investigate the Dyak trackers attached to the Army. A sergeant had been discovered on a troopship at Southampton with the shrunken head of a Chinese guerrilla in his kitbag. Every single time William talked about this Sophie would say: 'What do you mean "a Chinese guerrilla"! You mean the shrunken head of a Chinese teenager.' I could not sleep for days in thinking about that head. That beautiful Sunday William went on about someone called 'the odious General Templar.' Sophie wondered whether his reminiscences was REALLY due to his drinking. But she was back to her usual indirect self as she shook the malt beer tins very gently to make sure they are empty before throwing them away . . . with a THUD. I feel now that I should have gone for that walk with Melanie. Maybe there were boys sitting in FARQUHARSONS we could embarrass with our deliberate stares. I hope William never mentions that shrunken head again. I look at the sun, a small cloud is sliding across its face. I see the HEAD! Calm in death . . . relieved to done with Life — William looks up at the sky: 'Come on, lad, I dare you to shine! Five, four, three, two, one . . . zero! *(clapping)* That's it. SUMMER has returned!'

   Pop music

I had to put another record on. I had to turn up the quadrophonic sound. I had to absorb it into my bones. I had to close out everything. I had to live inside the sound . . . like being inside a huge breaker heading for a strange shore. William and Sophie are ruining my Summer today.

   She sits down

Barbara: Angkor, what AM I to tell your defence counsel . . . that you are completely mute, and maybe deaf . . . out of deliberation? What will they think of that? *(pause)* Maybe you want to be deported. You have become too sophisticated a young woman to be sent back to what was once your country. We do not know what is going on in Cambodia. There appears to be a complete news-blackout. We have no journalists there and can only rely on rumour. It is possible that complete city populations have been uprooted and sent to the rural areas. Sources say that the French-educated Cambodians are paying dearly for not having become revolutionaries. Angkor, there is no place for you there anymore. There is no comparative social grouping, which you are used to here, which you could join there. It is said that such groupings are being annihilated. *(loudly)* What WILL you do if you are deported! The Khmer Rouge will not accept you as you are . . . William and Sophie have seen to that. *(pause. quietly)* A highly conservative traditional society is being smashed to bits and ground up. Cambodia is entering the twentieth century by forced march. *(pause)*

(rising) I must go now, Angkor. I shall call back at the same time tomorrow. I am afraid tomorrow's visit must be the last. After that the Home Secretary's decision will be known with or without our influence. *(going towards her momentarily)* Won't you — *(she looks at* **Angkor** *a moment before going)*

Angkor: Some day people will look back on the twentieth century and say: 'How violent it all was! How did people survive?' Social history is my favourite subject at college. I had planned to study it at the best university available. William and Sophie would have helped me . . . maybe I will . . . somewhere —

Why is it that every small cloud in an otherwise empty sky must stick to the face of the sun like chocolate on a baby's face. William is waving his fist at this little cloud. I think he is slightly drunk. Sophie is pretending that nothing is happening. William complains that he has read an article twice without noticing because it is written in such an insipid style. He is bashing the Editorials, calling one 'a wankers' charter on Ulster' and another as 'the dead speaking for England again.' He has been commenting on a global scale since nine-o'clock this morning. Sophie stands back and looks at him with narrowed eyes in a doctorily fashion as he rants and raves at the end of his 'newspaper leash.' For a moment she puts her hand on his brow. He doesn't brush her hand away nor protest, but, actually calms down.

Things are silent except for the faint hum of a sleepy bee. I still can't stop looking at the sky for some reason. Then I notice this black object descending right above my head. It's a hawk . . . with rapidly beating wings it stays motionless in the sky. I wonder what it is looking at. What can there possibly be down here to eat — William, Sophie or me? Does that hawk see us as slightly, swaying carcass! What stops it from attacking any moving thing. I walk my fingers across the table. I swear I saw its eye flash in the sun. suddenly it drops like a stone behind the magnolia tree. I rush down the garden and stop and listen. But it is so quick I just have time to see it become a black object in the sky again.

William is asleep. I think he was done in by somebody's article on what David Frost thinks about Richard Nixon. William sees it as a CIA plot to bore the arse of the world . . . he is it's first victim. Sophie adjusts his straw hat over his face to prevent him from being burnt by the sun. Then she looks at me with a sigh of relief as if to say her troublesome baby has gone to sleep at last. I will take this opportunity to ask her a few questions that have been on my mind all morning. She immediately picks up a magazine as if she instinctively knew my intentions. I skateboard around and imagine myself a hawk hovering and waiting to sink my claws into something. Sophie, always a realist, yearns to get everything unpleasant over with as quickly as possible. She flings down the magazine and verbally goes to her corner like a boxer to await the bell. She starts talking about Melanie. I know she wonders why I haven't gone out with her today. It is not as if to say I was enjoying she and William's company today and can't pull myself away. Now I couldn't think of what I wanted to ask her. I don't know why I am hanging around this patio today.

About six swallows are in the sky . . . flying at speed, twisting and turning after one another like the latest jet fighters, letting out high-pitched cries. Sophie says I have an unusual interest in the sky. The sky is like the sea to me. It is an unfettered highway to anywhere in the world. How I wish I could see for hundreds of miles . . . even thousands instead of this goldfish view of the world. Sophie was still waiting for questions. I may as well think up a few more — like why was my name 'ANGKOR' and where did it originate? She looked at me as if I am a five year old asking my first question about birth and expecting to be told the story of the stork. 'Angkor was the ancient name for Cambodia. In A.D. Eleven Forty, under the rule of a powerful king named Suryavarman the Second —' I don't want an ancient name! I WANT my own name. Why should I have an ancient name . . . when all an ancient name can do is represent the ancient dead. Today in my country such ancient ideas are being throttled and bulldozed into the grave . . . She gave out a cry like an alarmed blackbird. I knew it was all over with Sophie and me. She was suddenly terrified of me. It was like the end of a love affair that I had once read about — one moment of terror can wreck years of love. It is possible to put one's finger on that moment like on a throbbing pulse and say: That was the moment that ended everything. For one moment the Truth was released from its cage and it wandered around and KILLED! She gently awakened William for assistance. I stood on my skateboard like a soldier directing traffic in a nation at war. William was finding it hard to awaken and focus on the real world. He had gone through a snorting, wide-open-mouthed-sleep and by now the beer must have turned to acid in his stomach. Sophie recovered enough to say: 'This IS your country, darling.' My language is coming back — I am sure that my language is coming back. 'But, darling, why bother you speak English so beautifully —' Sophie knew the battle was useless. William was wide enough awake now to be his old dismissive self — my language could be a second language but then it was difficult enough said he, glancing at Sophie, for one to get a word in edgeways in English never mind a second language.

I could feel nothing from them. It was worse than being alone. Only the presence of their flesh was holding up my thoughts like someone who occupies a telephone booth too long — it was that same sort of hatred that one can suddenly develop for total strangers.

A record of the BEACH BOYS plays. She listens a moment.

I looked out of my bedroom window down on to the patio and wondered what William and Sophie were saying about me. They were half-bent, leaning towards one another like two leaders of two super powers intent on being polite. I expect the Third World was undergoing some criticism. I turned up the quadrophonic and watched them shake their heads to show how disappointed they were in me. When I went down to the patio they were sitting united and respectable. William had neatly folded the 'Sundays' and Sophie had discarded the empty and . . . FULL malt beer tins. They greeted me politely and enquired after my health as if I were a terminal case of angina-pectoris. Obviously a new approach was going to be made towards this rather sad case of 'arrested dependence.' I had dutifully served my time as their child of conscience. NOW . . . what was to take me out of their orbit away from those second-hand shops that were supposed to aid the Third World. Once Sophie organized an 'Underdeveloped Ball'. Everyone was to arrive in newly bought second-hand clothes bearing something from their homes that they no longer wanted. I was dressed as Buddha with a piece of metallic-gold-painted cardboard strapped to my stomach — I think I represented 'DIGNITY'. For a long time afterwards I thought the Third World countries were dressed in old 'Marks and Sparks' trousers with woollen jumpers five times too big and carrying old radios, watches, cameras and meatgrinders that didn't work . . . with gold-metallic-painted cardboard strapped to their stomachs.

Sophie keeps asking me what I am thinking about: 'What is on your mind now, darling?' Then they sit pretending not to see me, but, when I fall off the skateboard William is up brushing me down lke a wire-haired terrier in order to dispel any suspicion of sensuality. William makes his apologies for having to go to the bathroom. When he is gone Sophie looks at me as if to say: 'Oh come on! Now's the time to tell me the truth.' Then she abruptly started to question me. It appears to be part of a strategy that she and William had worked out whilst I had been watching them from the window of my room. 'What was this sudden notion about country, language and hemisphere? Who was getting at me? Was it someone at school . . . a teacher, a student, a group? Some political organisation? Why could I not be just thoroughly at home? After all, I was so much a part of the country now. I had a good future. I was very intelligent and she was·sure that she and William had helped to bring out my potentiality. The only answer to this sudden inquisitiveness was that we should all travel to Thailand on Cambodia's border for a holiday this year . . . or next. THERE, I would find my curiosity satisfied without actually having to live out its consequences. No burnt boats or bridges, etc.' I started to wilt under her bombardment . . . I could only think of slogans to shout: Why did you name me 'ANGKOR'! I want to find my real name. My country is no longer called Cambodia — it is now Kampuchea. Where ARE my real parents! Why have I been stolen out of my country. Down with the baby snatchers! Down with the Petrilli Trust! She walked straight out of the patio as if she was off to fetch a straightjacket. I felt guilty about hurting Sophie. Her helplessness was agonising to watch. After a bit William arrived with an exaggerated relaxed walk, threw himself down like an old rag doll, put his feet up on the table and turned on his feline bitchiness. 'Damn it! Why don't we all go to — WHERE? Kampuchea. Here we are sitting under the sun while some poor bugger's getting backbreak and rheumatism standing up to his anus in damp water planting rice.' I didn't listen much to what he had to say after that. I was more attracted by a twin vapour trail which a tiny silver object was pulling across the sky like a diamond scratching glass. What were these planes that one could only see on beautiful days. The clouds in the sky must create the same effect as a warm sea drying up to reveal the snapping sharks on the seabed. I looked at William and realised he was still talking . . . saying inane things like: 'I don't know any English-educated Cambodians here in England except you . . . oh well, I suppose there must be some French-educated Cambodians from the old Protectorate living in exile in Paris — How's your French by the way?' He was being the perfect blue-moulded Occidental shit . . . as my Hong Kong science teacher said of people who displeased her.

I walked into the garden and sat down on the grass. The eyes of the forget-me-nots shone out of a patch of vivid blue. Tell me what to do. I sit here on this beautiful sunny Sunday . . . WAITING. I do not know why except that I must wait.

Sophie joined William eventually. I knew she had been crying. I went up to her and put my hand gently on her cheek. She has beautiful skin and I told her so. I even kissed William on the cheek. He was so happy! He went into the house and put on Brahms First Symphony Final Movement . . . very loud.

the record plays

Sophie and I walked around the garden arm in arm. Then William suggested that we play a game of putting. It was at the third hole that a huge shadow fell on the grass.

She looks up quickly as a low-flying jet screams overhead.

Run, run, they're going to kill us! I crawl into a bamboo grove and hide. Through a hole I see the silver planes dropping out of the sky . . . everything is burning. A water buffalo ablaze with napalm is setting the undergrowth on fire as it tries to escape. Some huge trucks arrive. Soldiers get out and set fire to the rest of the houses. A bulldozer digs a hole for the bodies . . . those who are alive are dragged on to the lorries tied up like chickens. Before the trucks drive off I hear a voice crying out. It is my father. 'Poi, Poi! Kill them . . . Kill them, Poi!' I run to the forest and dig up the gun. It is too heavy . . . the trigger is too stiff! It is too HEAVY! NO! It is light! Why has it become light?

> *Two shots ring out.*

Barbara *(entering quickly):* Good morning, Angkor.

Angkor: I am Poi.

Barbara: WELL . . . I AM glad that we are going to talk today. It is so near the time. One question: Do you have any recollection of shooting your foster-parents? *(pause)* They dug up an army-issue browning pistol belonging to William. Do you remember burying it under the magnolia tree?

You are being held in detention pending the Home Secretary's decision on your deportation. Angkor, do you know where you are? Please try and remember.

> *She repeats this speech over and over again in a low voice.*

Angkor *(to herself):* I remember . . . Poi remembers.

> *A choir of children sing an Asian song.*

BLACKOUT